AGING
IN PLACE

AGING IN PLACE

5 Steps to Designing a Successful Living Environment for Your Second Half of Life

AARON D. MURPHY

ENTREPRENEUR
PUBLISHING

For permission requests, please address
Entrepreneur Publishing
PO Box 2222
Poulsbo, WA 98370

Published 2014 by Entrepreneur Publishing
Printed in the United States of America

18 17 16 15 14   1 2 3 4 5

ISBN 978-1-936672-63-9

Library of Congress Control Number: 2014931320

I dedicate this book to my parents, Stephen and Carol Murphy. They have been my support since birth, and the strength of that support has never waned.

I also dedicate this book to my children, Noah and Paige Murphy. My drive and passion for what I do is innately and intimately intertwined with my desire to support you both in the best way I know how and am capable of at any given moment in time.

I constantly strive to find new ways to show you how much I love you both, and I hope that I can live a life you will both be proud to be associated with. I hope that through my own passionate pursuits I am able to create results in my life both professionally and as a hands-on parent, that you can look back on as adults and say "Wow, Dad really worked hard and he really cared about us and loved us through it all"—just like my parents did for me.

"I've learned that people will forget what you said, people will forget what you did, but people will never forget how you made them feel."
—Maya Angelou

Contents

Introduction:

THERE ARE SEVEN HUNDRED MILLION Americans just like you, looking for answers about "aging in place." Answers to what your future looks like. Answers to what it looks like in relation to your health, your happiness, your newfound longevity, and how to stay in your own home and community as long as you possibly can. That's why we wrote this book, for you.

I am an architect and the son of two baby boomers who were born in 1950. By definition, boomers are those born between 1946 and 1964. My grandmother went through all the challenges of aging in a split-level style '70s home, and it didn't work for her. While she deteriorated physically from osteoporosis, and mentally, through the phases of Alzheimer's, my family tried to meet those challenges for her in a home that couldn't possibly accommodate her needs. I don't want you to have to struggle like our family did, without the information and resources that are available today.

I practice architecture in Washington State, and my industry has changed more drastically during the last several years than anyone currently practicing architecture can remember. A few major factors have radically altered our industry. First is the current economy, with the housing crash and a multiple-year real estate fallout that started in 2007. Add to that the stock market crash that occurred in 2008-09, along with the continuation of lending debacles that took place in the United States and abroad. These woes have created a "perfect storm" that I hope we never have to repeat.

Being in an industry over the last few years that has financing and housing (with historic record-setting declines) as the book ends that hold it up, I am one of many in the building and design industry who has been looking for the new "normal." As an entrepreneur and the owner of a small architecture firm, I found myself looking for opportunities to reinvent some portion of my business model. It was time to look deep inside, and also to be willing to think "outside the box." How could I differentiate myself? What was my real passion, and how did that relate to my industry? Was there a role of "servant leadership" that I could fill and be proud of? How could my passion set me apart? How could I be unique as an architect and leverage my strengths and skills?

My reflections took me back 15 to 20 years, to my time in college at the University of Washington.

I remember going home to the Portland/Vancouver area quarterly to visit my parents, typically tackling the

MaryJo Murphy 1921-2000 Carl Murphy, 1920 -

three-hour drive with the back seat of my car full of laundry. As often as possible, I made sure that I visited my paternal grandparents as well. We had a wonderful and supportive family as I was growing up, all living in the Portland area. We all got together weekly when I was younger. As aunts and uncles got jobs in other cities in the northwest, the family still managed monthly get-togethers for a day of visiting and a potluck style meal. My father's parents (my grandparents) were the hub of the family for decades.

The challenge in going home three or four times a year during my college and architecture studies was in watching my grandmother change over those years. Mary Jo Murphy was once a bright and postured lady of five foot nine who, in her retirement, traveled the world as a Masters-level bridge (cards) player. While I was away at school, she deteriorated into a hunched over version of her former self, at only five foot two and trapped in a hospital bed in her living room, unaware of who her caregiver, my grandfather, was.

In this period of time my grandmother was taken from our family via the onslaught of osteoporosis and eventually Alzheimer's disease. With each visit, I saw a new phase in her deterioration. She went from walking upright to using a cane, then a walker, and eventually a wheel-chair. Her emotional makeup took the same downward spiral. She was a challenge to be around during those last few years of her cognitive awareness. She became impa-tient, explosive, and downright mean at times. It was a struggle for our family as a whole, and it aged my grand-father tremendously. Finally, for her last two years or so, she was simply "present" physically, but nowhere to be found mentally. She was brought to family gatherings, but she was not in any way aware or coherent. My grand-father went through all the phases with her, as a devoted Roman Catholic, in the true vein of "until death do us part." He cared for her in the beginning when her needs were fairly minor. Then a friend from her card-playing circles took on the role as a paid assistant. Eventually, around the clock in-home medical care was arranged to meet all of her needs. This care included every "activity of daily living" (referred to as "ADLs" by occupational therapists), like feeding, dressing, and bathing.

As a young aspiring architect in my early twenties, I wasn't ready to learn about all the physical aspects of my grandmother's deterioration, nor the medical needs of her daily life. I didn't want to know. At my age then, it was too hard to think about. But what I did notice, based on what I was learning in school, was that their 1970's split-level home was *broken*. The design didn't work for her at all. In a split-level home like theirs, the laundry room is one-half of a flight downstairs from the front door. All of the restrooms, bathing facilities, and

bedrooms were up another flight of stairs. Only the living room, dining room, and kitchen were on the main living floor where you enter the house. From the driveway, it was necessary to climb some exterior stairs to the front porch deck, due to the slope of the land. *None* of this worked for my grandmother the moment that her needs started to change!

That is what I noticed at the time. And that is what I recalled in the spring of 2009, when pondering what I could offer as an architect in the current economy.

Another piece of the puzzle that led me to write this book came in an "aha" moment in 2009. My 1995 Toyota Camry, a graduation present from my folks, finally died in the spring of 2009. I enjoyed riding a scooter until we hit the normal November weather in Seattle. The fun was over! I found a 1993 Ford Taurus on Craigslist and negotiated an offer. At the test drive, I met the couple who were selling the car, both around my parents' age, 60 to 65. They told me that this had been their mother's vehicle. They'd finally convinced their 94-year-old mom to hang up her keys! Knowing the county well, I asked where she lived. They named a local assisted-living facility along one of the many waterfront stretches of land we're so blessed to have here. I'd been thinking about how my grandmother's house failed to serve her needs, and about the costs and timing of those tough decisions about elder care. I got up the gumption to ask what it cost for her to live there. My jaw dropped in shock: It cost them $150,000 out of pocket to enroll, and from *$6,000-8,000 per month!* This gave her a single-room unit and the care program that she needed based on her situation and age.

I was astounded. I remember commenting to them, "I know my 401K is now a 201K after the recent stock market plummet—so who can afford *that*?" They simply shrugged their shoulders and forced a smile.

So those were the two experiences that led me to this point. First, my family's ordeal with a home that couldn't function for my grandmother as her physical and cognitive needs changed. And second, a story about how completely unaffordable the facility style choices appear to be for any average American family with a normal working household income.

It was time to find solutions and opportunities to help people. I was driven to find out how I could leverage my education, professional experience, and my values and skills to best help the average American family make their home living environments work better as their "forever home." My goal was clear. I wanted to allow you to stay in your home longer, be happier, and have your house work the way you need it to as your needs change with age. This was my new-found passion in residential architecture—and my calling. It was the inspiration that I needed to achieve my "Certified Aging-In-Place Specialist" classification through the National Association of Home Builders & AARP program at the end of 2009.

Seventy million people will be turning 65 years old over the next two or three decades, and I want to enable these people to stay in their own homes. I have been tackling this challenge in a big way. Every day I'm helping people just like you to navigate the process and solutions for successful aging in place.

Chapter One:

What's Happening to Our Population? Is Housing Ready?

OUR WORLD IS CHANGING DRASTICALLY right now. There is something crashing upon our shores here in the United States and abroad as well. It's called the "Silver Tsunami." This refers to the fact that as of January 2011, there are 10,000 people are turning age 65 *every single day*. That is *one new 65-year-old every eight seconds*! The population "triangle" as it used to be called, wherein the bulk of our population is weighted more heavily in younger age groups than in the older ones, has just recently become inverted for the first time in the history of our civilization.

Here are some additional statistics to help you wrap your head around the size of the challenges that lie ahead:

- 77 million people were born between 1946 and 1964, which is defined as the baby boomer era (U.S. Census).

- The senior age group is now, for the first time, the largest in terms of size and percent of the population in the U.S. This age group grew at a faster rate than the total population between 2000 and 2010, according to a 2010 Census brief.

- More people were 65 years and over in 2010 than in any previous census. Between 2000 and 2010, the population 65 years and over increased at a faster rate (15.1%) than the total U.S population (9.7%).

- By 2015, those aged 50 and older will represent 45% of the U.S. population (AARP).

- Baby Boomers make up 35% of the American adult population (Scarborough).

- By 2030, the 65-plus population will double to about 71.5 million, and by 2050 will grow to 86.7 million people (U.S. Census).

- In 2050, the number of Americans aged 65 and older is projected to be 88.5 million, more than double its projected population of 40.2 million in 2010.

- Between 1950 and 2040, the percentage of 80+ year olds will increase from 0.5 percent of our U.S. population to 5 percent.

That is a *tenfold* increase in that portion of our demographic population, and most of it will occur in the next 30 years!

http://www.immersionactive.com/resources/50-plus-facts-and-fiction/

Couple these statistics with the fact that our longevity has increased more in the last 100 years than it did in the previous 5,000 years of civilization, due to advances in western medicine and technology. And now we've got an issue that needs some serious attention. Since the industrial revolution, we've added 30 years to our life expectancy—and all of this has occurred in the lifetime of my own 93-year-old grandfather! Advancements in

Figure 2.
Population by Age and Sex: 2000 and 2010
(For information on confidentiality protection, nonsampling error, and definitions, see *www.census.gov/prod/cen2010/doc/sf1.pdf*)

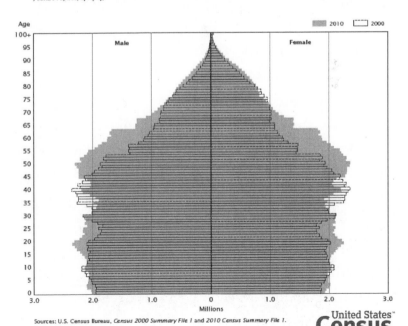

Sources: U.S. Census Bureau, *Census 2000 Summary File 1* and *2010 Census Summary File 1*.

United States
Census
Bureau

medicine and technology over this past century have been truly astounding, in everything from evaluation and diagnosis to surgeries and pharmaceutical options. We should be proud of our advancements in these industries. But the implications of this newly-found longevity pose huge challenges to come. Just think that in the history of humankind, two-thirds (67 percent) of all the people who lived to be 65 years old *are alive today*! This clearly suggests that we are heading for a new era, a place we've never been before as a nation.

As a licensed architect, I am acutely aware of how those challenges will impact my own industry. There will be an astounding amount of pressure put on the existing housing stock of our nation. Supply and demand expectations will make a significant shift that will affect the next wave of future housing development, home remodeling solutions, and the buyers of the existing housing stock that is available for the next three to four buying cycles. "Boomer consumers" will be at the helm of decision making: by their sheer numbers, and because of their wealth. Boomers have approximately *five times* the net worth (read into that "purchasing power" or "disposable income") compared to the average income in the United States! Are we paying attention? I think we're starting to, but I'm not sure it's quickly enough or seriously enough.

Neighborhoods are changing in ways we may not be prepared for with such a significant alteration in the "buyer pool" and their needs over the next 20 to 30 years. Based on a seven-year average of home ownership, this means three to four home purchasing decisions for the average U.S. family.

Consider this: **Two-thirds of "Suburbia" has now been "empty-nested."** The kids have gone off to college or otherwise moved out and moved on. The structure of the individual house and the neighborhood as a whole isn't functioning any longer in a way that suits the current occupants or the next few buyers of these homes. **That statistic of empty-nested homes will soon be at 75 percent.** Three out of every four of those 2,400+ square foot, 3-4 bedroom, 2+ bathroom homes are now occupied by only two people.

Longevity Is Opportunity:
Riding the Demographic Wave

http://www.milkeninstitute.org/events/gcprogram.taf?function=
detail&eventid=gc13&EvID=4079

And those home-owners are getting older, less able to navigate the stairs of that two-story "spec" (speculative) built house that maximized the square footage on the minimum developers' lot size. When a builder or developer takes that approach—-to get the most lots and houses (sellable units) in a subdivision—-he has likely created mostly two-story homes, all with interior stairs. He has also likely created a situation on the lot where you need at least a few stairs to reach the front door, or to get from the garage to the main floor living spaces.

These homes also have code minimum hallway and

door widths that are too narrow for our future needs. A "spec house" is ideally suited to be easy to use for anyone who is able-bodied and "typical" in every way: height, weight, eyesight, hearing, verbal communication, and the like. Does that sound like a housing solution that will meet the massively increasing "boomer bulge" of buyers looking for their final or "forever home" to suit their needs in the decades ahead? No, I don't think so either.

At some level, "Suburbia" is over. Originally those neighborhoods and the sprawl that occurred was due to the beginnings of a two-car society, dual career and income families, and the desire for housing to be separated from commercial districts, and centered around schooling facilities instead of commerce. That is no longer the right solution for the largest and fastest growing sectors of our U.S. demographic over the next 30 years.

So the situation with this aging population will involve drastic adjustments, innovation, and new solutions in a multitude of industries. It requires a *paradigm shift*. The housing industry is just one of the industries at stake, and it will most definitely need solutions that are integrated with the industries of medicine, health care, transportation, and social services (among others) in order to effectively meet the needs of the changing consumer makeup in the decades ahead. Are we ready to take on the challenge? I sure hope so! I know that thought leaders in these industries are all loudly pushing the same message to the public as the Silver Tsunami comes crashing upon our shores: *"Paddle faster*!"

So let's take a look at this epidemic on a personal level. Let's see how we can make sure you don't get stuck in the pain and fear of the unknown the way my grandmother did in her broken home. *Let's empower you to be in control of your future, your personal solution, your living environment, and your forever home!*

Chapter Two:

What Does Successful "Aging In Place" Look Like?

LET'S START HIGH AT A 50,000 foot level and address the basics and background information that you'll need. Then we can dive down and zoom in from there.

What is "Aging In Place"?

We've defined aging in place in our own words, as the concept that you can and should be able to stay in your residence or current living situation, or chose the location of your residence and your community, for the remainder of your life. This should be true regardless of your physical, cognitive, or other abilities, and your income and financial situation.

AARP explains it in a bit more of a communal sense here:

The vast majority of older adults want to age in place, so they can continue to live in their own homes or communities. As the older population grows, the degree to which it can participate in community life and reach needed services will be determined, in part, by how communities are designed. This report examines state policies that can help older adults age in place. These policies include integrating land use, housing and transportation; efficiently delivering services in the home; providing more transportation choices, particularly for older adults who no longer drive; and improving affordable, accessible housing to prevent social isolation.

http://assets.aarp.org/rgcenter/ppi/liv-com/ib190.pdf

AARP goes on to comment that *"Nearly 90 percent of people over age 65 want to stay in their home for as long as possible, and 80 percent believe their current residence is where they will always live. However, for older adults to age in place, their physical and service environment must be accommodating."*

Who is the world around us designed for?

Most people go through their daily lives without being aware that the man-made world around us, in general, has been designed for: **able-bodied, right-handed** *young adults of average height, average weight, perfect sight and perfect hearing, along with the ability to verbally communicate their needs to another human being.*

Does this definition fit you? How about your parents? If it does define you correctly now, will it in another 5, 10, or 20 years? It's doubtful, on at least one if not multiple counts. How many elderly people can expect to continue to function as truly "normal," by this definition, through the end of their days?

Successful aging in place requires design solutions to be customized and client-driven. Good design should be specific to each client's personal situation and challenges, along with their own specific wants and needs.

This is proven by the fact that the *multi-billion dollar industry* of assisted-living facilities openly admits that they are capturing only 5 to 8 percent of their target demographic. Why do you think this is so? It's because *we don't want to live there*! Not as our first choice, anyway. The other *700 million* people in the United States want to *stay in their own homes* as a first preference, and for as long as they can remain there happily and independently.

The Big Boom Theory:
What The Boomer Consumer Wants
http://eventcallregistration.com/reg/index.jsp?cid=31562t11

Even when people are confronted with the idea that they may need help with some of the tasks and activities of daily living ("ADLs" as they are termed by the occupational therapy industry) such as cooking, cleaning, shopping, and eventually dressing and bathing — 82 percent of those polled still say that they would like to remain in their own homes during that phase of their lives as well. We don't argue *if* the assisted-living facility solution has a place on the continuum of the caretaking spectrum. Rather, we ask: *when* is the right time for it? Polls tell us quite clearly that the vast majority of our adults answer this question with one word: *later.*

Places that used to be known as "old folks homes" are now called "continuing care retirement communities" or CCRCs by the healthcare industry. Increasingly, the average American simply can't afford the entrance costs and monthly fees for these campus-style facilities that provide on-site, all-inclusive solutions for every housing, health, dining, and medical need of every individual at the facility.

As an advocate for aging in place, I teach, present, and network with all kinds of people. And I hear hundreds of personal stories about people dealing with aging relatives and care facilities. Many of the stories I've heard about moving someone into a facility setting are tainted with sadness and disappointment. Some of the stories are truly devastating. I've heard about vibrant individuals who became depressed and reclusive, and even a few who have committed suicide. But of course this isn't everyone's story. I have also heard some great success stories about elders who thrive with the engagement and social interaction in these facilities and older community homes.

Whatever the public perception of "institutionalized" housing in the latter part of life, there is enough statistical support about our personal preferences and biases to underscore that we want to make our own houses our *homes* for as long as it is reasonable to stay there safely. It's where we love, it's where we know, and it's where we are happiest. We don't like change, especially related to our living environments. So it makes sense to invest the effort needed to help us remain where we want to be.

I've been fortunate to be a part of the design and construction drawings for over one million square feet of commercial architectural projects. These public spaces, by code requirements and building regulations, require an adherence to standards that allow "accessibility for all" via the American Disabilities Act (ADA). This is to accommodate people in wheelchairs and with other ambulatory differences than the typical person.

With this background, I'm inherently skewed toward a belief in equal access for everyone. I have decades of experience that lend themselves very well to bringing those ideas and solutions into the realm of *residential* architecture—-where there isn't that inherent belief (or the current code requirement support) to make sure that homes are livable for everyone, regardless of their physical ability.

Beyond the million plus square feet of commercial design experience, I've recently been on a design team for two different 100,000+ square foot hotels in the Seattle area. Over the months of designing and redesigning these facilities, I learned how best to design any multi-unit housing structure *from the developer and owner's perspective.* Modularity in design with a focus on only a few repeating unit (room) types, mirrored unit floor plans, and maximum efficiencies are the key. The key to what, you might ask. The key (in these repetitions, efficiencies, and minimal alterations to the unit layouts) is to quickly get to full occupancy, and therefore, profitability. That's fine for this building and facility type, but it's exactly why we don't want to live there. There *is not anything* about how a senior housing facility is designed (in the continuum of care such as assisted-living, nursing home, etc.) that is specifically about *you.*

Yes, design does consider older people if it's a CCRC type building like assisted-living or a nursing home. And there are ADA and other accessibility and medical design solutions to suit the standard and typical types of people who use and occupy the facility. But my point is that it lacks an individualized and personal solution. A facility's unit layout doesn't take into consideration *your* needs and *your* challenges; nor does it meet *your specific desires* for a housing solution. It can't, because they've never even *met you*! **Our stance on aging in place is that it requires teamwork; it's about having a personal relationship with your design team, and**

together coming up with a specifically personal and client-driven solution.

Having a "personal design team" is a critical piece of successful aging in place. You need someone who has been at your dining room table, walked through your home with you, and is actively listening. A good designer will take the time to build rapport and to understand your situation, your personal wants, needs, and rights. It's best to find a professional who is accessible to you—-in person and by phone. The planning process will involve interviews with you and likely other family members as well, about your current and future needs, based on your specific personal situation. The better your designer understands this information, the better he or she can design your customized and personal solution for aging in place. A good architect and home designer will be able to "read between the lines" as well. They'll hear you talk about your financial situation, your desires, and even your fears. They will talk to you. They will listen to you. They will design a solution that fits *you*.

That's why I am sharing the information in this book, and why I started www.EmpoweringTheMatureMind. com. My design team is dedicated to helping you stay in your own home if that's what you desire. **We want you to maintain your independence, keep your family, keep your pet, be able to continue to play in your garden and remain surrounded by your own belongings, memories, support network, and community for as long as humanly possible.**

SUCCESS STORY:

I was contacted by a man who owns a local franchise that offers in-home non-medical care for older Americans. He told me that he'd passed on my business card to long-time friends of his whom we'll call Bill and Clara. They had remodeled parts of their home, but still needed help with their kitchen, dining room, and home office. Clara contacted me, and I met with them to discuss the project. Bill and Clara are wonderful people, full of energy, and very set on staying active and involved in their community and their family's lives.

Nine years ago, Clara completed a bike ride across America. But within the last few years, she'd had a minor stroke, and she was having trouble with her grip. Therefore, maneuvering dishes and preparing food were a particular challenge for her that we wanted to over-come with our design solution. Also, high storage was a problem since Clara was five foot three, and she strug-gled to reach for items in the upper cabinetry—in both her kitchen and her office.

Between their good communication about their own specific wants and needs, and my experience as a CAPS architect, we were able to work very effectively together and design a solution for each of these areas in their home.

Clara's renovated office workspace had dimensions created specifically for her height, reach, and grip abili-ties. Both work surface and upper shelving were set at non-standard heights to fit her needs. In the new kitchen, her dishes were relocated into lower drawers for heavier items. We made upper cabinetry that "pulled down" toward the counter height for those items that needed to be accessed daily. We also designed together for a drawer-style dishwasher located near the main kitchen sink to facilitate the way they washed the dishes. We added a few small, sturdy step stools that popped out of toe-kick locations under the base cabinets, just below upper cabinets that had things Clara needed to reach. We also added a prep sink with cutting board, and were able to build the island she'd always wanted. We kept and reused most of the custom glasswork shelves Bill had designed, incorporating those into an under-counter lighted display for their family photos.

For future planning, we allowed the main sink to have under-counter cabinet doors that were attached to the toe-kick space, so that the base cabinet doors, when opened, would allow for "roll-in" access via wheelchair or other mobility device. This option keeps the kitchen functioning well for any and all users, both now and into the future.

This project and design was a complete success. It allowed an older couple (in their late sixties, early seventies) to resolve the current challenges they were facing in using their home. As a team of client and architect, we created customized, personal solutions that make their home work better now with a plan for the future as well. We created spaces they can use effectively, since they both want to remain in this home for the rest of their lives, in the house and community they love.

So this book is for the 700 million or so older Americans who would like to age in place, remaining in the residence of their choice versus having to move into a facility of some sort before they are ready or willing to do so. Now let's walk through five steps down the path for a successful journey toward aging in place.

Chapter Three:

Starting the Discussion

"Don't wait. The time will never be just right."
—Napoleon Hill

IT TAKES TIME. When we give presentations to educate the public on aging in place, most folks are typically in denial—at least, subconsciously. We're discussing morbidity and mortality, and nobody likes to talk about getting older.

Recently, Hillary Clinton was in the hospital to remove a blood clot from behind her right ear. She had had the stomach flu; she got dehydrated, got dizzy, slipped and fell, and hit her head. The Forbes' second most powerful woman in the world in 2012 slipped, fell, and hit her head. And she was *home alone*. The outcome could have turned out much worse, and we're grateful it didn't. But it can happen to anybody, at any time, in a split second—possibly altering the victim's capabilities permanently and changing the course of their lives.

That's why we suggest that you start the discussion now with your own family members. Start this discussion with **yourself**. It takes multiple visits to the issues and a gentle and relaxed approach over time. Only then will you get to the point where you are having honest and sincere conversations with yourself and your family on what is best for you, and how to fix your home to stay there if that is your goal.

I talk about communication around this topic in some of our blogs and articles online at EmpoweringTheMatureMind.com. If at all possible, start the discussion *before an emergency,* so you can take the appropriate time and tact to do it correctly, greatly increasing the likelihood of a successful outcome with your loved ones.

I understand the challenge of bringing up this topic. It is one of the toughest things that we will ever deal with. No one wants to admit that we are getting older or less capable or less independent—let alone that we should plan for it in advance. But how many other things do we knowingly plan and prepare for in our lives? We plan ahead for retirement. We plan ahead to fund our children's college education. We plan ahead when purchasing health and life insurance policies. In these scenarios that we are all accustomed to, it's simply *a part of life* to plan ahead and prepare.

Aging is a part of life too. Aging will change the housing needs for each and every one of us. We have just never, as a nation, had to address this topic in relation to such a massive percentage of our population! And the discussion is creating new terminology among many industries.

In one of my blog entries, I reference an excellent interview online by David Solie, talking to LivHOME co-founder Mr. Steve Barlam, about what the aging in place industry refers to as "in home care." Mr. Barlam makes some excellent points and provides great insight and tips on how to approach the conversation with a parent about the beginning of (and transition toward) needing some help at home to maintain their independence. In-home care, likely to be needed eventually, can be an important aspect of successful aging in place. There is a large breadth of services that in home care agencies can provide, and their services should cater to the individual, just like home design should. Depending on the agency, the state they practice in, and the licensing they have, they can provide everything from companionship and socialization all the way to hospice care.

SUCCESS STORY:

On the Internet radio show that I co-host, we recently had a wonderful guest on the air who is a franchise owner of an in home care agency named Comfort Keepers. Carol told a story about a client we'll call Mary, and how Comfort Keepers was able to assist Mary in ways that her spouse and family could not. Mary's children lived far away and her husband's physical abilities were waning. Comfort Keepers provided hospice care for her, and

Mary had such great experiences with the caregivers in that final year of her life.

In another instance, Comfort Keepers was able to give an older spouse a weekly *break* from caring for his wife who had dementia. Then he could regularly go have lunch with his buddies and get some personal time and space during this caretaking challenge he had lovingly committed himself to. He told his wife that he had his weekly "meeting" to go to, and when he left, the caregivers gave his wife her weekly "spa treatment." They washed her hair and did her nails and makeup while he enjoyed some social time away. When he returned, he always told her how beautiful she looked and how lucky he was to have her! This arrangement became an important ritual for both the wife and the husband, and it strengthened their bond in these latter years of her life.

Some clients' experience with palliative care, even prior to hospice care, is so successful that they end up improving enough to move "backwards" on the continuum of the agency's care offerings.

** You can hear this story by using this URL link for further details: http://www.blogtalkradio.com/encoreliving/2013/05/07/encore-living—why-home-care-is-not-a-luxury

DISCUSSIONS WITH OUR PARENTS

Talking to our parents about their futures and their changing abilities related to age is one of the most challenging conversations and delicate topics we'll face in our adult lives as "children." Steve Barlam, LivHOME co-founder, speaks about the importance of *planning ahead*. He mentions ideas like the "pacing of the conversation" over an extended period of time. I can't stress strongly enough the need to initiate this *before* an acute occurrence such as a fall or an illness.

As with any relationship, being a good listener and bringing a caring approach to the conversation is critical. Don't be in a hurry to reach conclusions. This takes gentle exploration over time. Spend enough time in conversation engaging the other person to get to the root of their *fears, wants, and needs for the future*. The more you understand their perspectives, wishes, and opinions, the better aligned you'll be with their goals. Then you can address those goals in coordination with your own thoughts and ideas. As you maintain patience, courtesy, and respect for your loved one, over time you will become a "trusted adviser." This role allows you to facilitate open conversations about new or potential future realities that lead to acceptance and open up the possibilities and benefits of planning for those changes.

Without this careful approach to the conversation with your loved one, the likely result will be a natural human instinct of push back, a checkmate, and the knee-jerk reaction of "*No!*" None of us wants this outcome. This is why I've included this valuable information about an approach that can result in a much more positive outcome for all parties involved.

So, to use Mr. Barlam's vocabulary: Which type of communicator are you in relation to your loved one?

And, should you consider changing that category?

1) The Retreater: This person avoids conflict and either can't seem to bring up the conversation at all or immediately backs off when any sign of resistance arises, dropping the conversation until "next time." This approach will result in the eventual "acute occurrence" (such as a parent or spouse falling and breaking a hip), requiring one to now step into action *in panic mode*, without any information about what the wants and needs of the injured person are. This is not a good situation to be in. These discussions need to take place before something happens that forces you into a panic mode. It's time to step up and address the future while you can do so pro-actively, in *planning mode*. You'll be glad you did.

2) The Bulldozer: These people have no time for this! They are impatient and need decisions *right now*. They are decision makers, which can be positive in many situations—but not in this one. We have a natural tendency to push back when being told what to do. You don't like it, and neither will your parent or loved one, especially when discussing their diminishing abilities or independence! This is the communication style that can ruin relationships or at least result in that stalemate we are trying to avoid.

3) The Engager: This is the winning approach and the type of communicator you should work toward becoming in addressing this delicate and potentially volatile topic. This takes patience, respect, courtesy, a gentle delivery, and an allowance to let the conversation unfold over an extended period of time. As is frequently the case in life, the most challenging road is the right one to reach your destination. This approach requires that you allow your parent or loved one, who's likely to be skeptical, to gain the trust that you have their best interest in mind. It requires that you allow them to express their fears and concerns while you take the time to actively listen. Even with all these requirements, it's a worthwhile goal toward a worthwhile destination. You'll have a loved one who is willing to listen to you as well, to hear about your hopes, thoughts, and feelings. You'll reach a destination where your parent or partner can accept a future that could look different than the present in regards to their own life, independence, and some freedoms.

Recently I participated in the Urban Land Institute (ULI) conference in our county, titled "Building Better Neighborhoods." I was one of four speakers that morning over breakfast, to a room of over 250 industry colleagues including city mayors, planners, developers, city and county council folks, as well as commissioners, real estate agents, builders, and the like. As the last speaker before the panel Q&A session, I asked the emcee ahead of time if he minded that I "wake people up a bit." He shared my sense of humor, so I went for it. As I climbed the two or three steps up to the platform with the podium,

I tripped—on purpose—and fell! Pens and papers I had in hand went flying as I disappeared behind the podium, making a huge thud as I hit the platform floor. All of the women gasped! Likely some of the men were whispering "What an idiot" under their breath. I stood up, leaned into the microphone, and asked, "Did that scare you?" From the female contingent, primarily, came an astounding flood of "Yes!"

"You don't even know me," I said. "What if that was *your mother* who fell today while you were at work?" I let them sit with the silence for an uncomfortable amount of time. "The moment that happens, you don't have time to hire me," I explained. "During the six to eight weeks your mom is in the hospital for hip surgery, moved to a rehab and physical therapy facility, and eventually discharged back to her home, you can't hire me, do a design, get a permit, find a contractor, and do a construction project. But when your mom returns home, her needs are going to be different than they were before she fell. That's why I'm here today speaking to you." And on I went with my presentation, which ended with a standing ovation.

For successful aging in place, we need to *plan ahead*. It starts with initiating conversations with our family and loved ones. We need to be having these conversations *now*.

Here are some practical and realistic suggestions for how to start the conversation. The "soft startup" conversation ideas here will vary slightly depending on who you are talking with: a spouse, a parent, or a friend. Regardless, the ideas and general structure of how to open the topic are applicable in all scenarios.

Some possible prompts:

"Dad, I've been thinking a lot about you lately. I love you, and I'm worried about something. I'd like to share this with you, if that's all right."

"Sweetheart, I have been thinking a lot about us—-and about you. I love you, and I want to share some thoughts, as I really need your input on some important issues I have mulling around in my head. Is this a good time to talk?"

"Mom, I haven't seen you in a while, and I've been losing sleep the last few weeks thinking about you. I really love you, and I want to talk with you—-so I can appease my own concerns. Can I ask a few questions I've been wondering about?"

"Honey, I've been stressed out recently. I have some feelings and concerns that I can't get out of my head related to your safety. Can I share my feelings with you?"

"Mom, I know I can't be here with you and for you all the time when you need someone, and that makes me sad sometimes. I worry about it, and I worry about you because I love you so much. I probably don't need to worry, but I can't help it. I want the best for you, and I need to share a few things I've been thinking about recently. Is that all right with you?"

Starting a conversation without being confrontational accomplishes several things. It can create a gentle and subconscious shift in the relationship that brings you closer to becoming (1) an equal, if you are the child, and (2) a trusted adviser further down the road. That is a great goal to work toward. And it is totally legitimate to open the conversation for the sake of *your own peace of mind* that your loved one can continue to be safe, happy, and independent. **Partnering is empowering for both parties. And it's a true *win-win* discussion if it's done right.**

Chapter Four:

Being an <u>Active</u> Listener

ACTIVE LISTENING IS a communication skill that requires the listener to give their undivided attention to the speaker, refrain from interrupting, occasionally ask relevant questions for further information, and summarize or paraphrase (in their own words) what they have heard back to the speaker. Thus, the listener confirms the speaker's meaning and, hopefully, the feeling behind the words as well.

My father preaches active listening as a priceless asset in business, and he's an absolute master at it. His ability to listen has a lot to do with his business success and the client loyalty he has created over his own 40+ years in business. It's his honest and sincere interest in what they are saying, and his ability to feed that back to them, followed by his own curious questions about what they just finished saying. Honestly, it's incredible to watch.

When people interact with the pace of life these days, they are often simply "waiting to speak" rather than listening attentively. Listeners are often distracted or otherwise consumed by their own thoughts and mental activities. Active listening is a disciplined and structured way of listening and responding to others. It requires sincerity and focus, and increases the listener's awareness of the other person, while inviting responses that are notably more honest, less subjective, and more productive toward an end goal or solution.

This is the idea in a nutshell. But it requires some elaboration for the sake of truly wrapping your head around the concept.

Have you ever heard the phrase "the truth is three levels deep"? I feel that this is the way of getting to the real answers, which will include those desires, needs, and especially the fears (real or perceived) associated with the client's outlook of the future. It will require many visits to a conversation, as previously stated, to uncover this critical truth layer. Active listening requires much more than simply nodding your head and thinking about what you want to say next. You'll be paying attention to the nuance, the intonation, and the body language of the story being told to you—in addition to the words themselves. That is where the truth lies.

There is another reason the "three levels deep" issue is pertinent. It requires that you've spent enough time and engagement with the other person to have gained the *trust and rapport* necessary for them to feel comfortable sharing their real truths and fears about a situation. You need that especially in this arena, where your goal is to help someone you love (or whom I want to help as a client in my case). If your goal is to find the best solution for aging in place for someone, you have to log the time and provide the undivided attention that they need from you in order to receive real and honest information that you need from them. There are no shortcuts to this process.

So take the time. Seek the truth. Find the answers and solutions that only come from "peeling back the onion" in layers over time and multiple visits to the topic of conversation. To prevent the scenario of being forced into this conversation while in a reactive panic mode, *you must be proactive and plan ahead.* Start this conversational journey before it's required and needed "yesterday." Start it now.

I've read some amazing books over the last 20 years. One that I found fascinating was a sales book I read while purchasing single family homes as a full time real estate investing venture for a few years. This book honed my abilities and skills for connecting with people and conveying my desire to create a win-win solution for them with their housing situations. As the owner of **Silver Lining Properties, LLC** (*"Creating Win/Win Real Estate Solutions"*), I needed to learn to create with others, as quickly as humanly possible, the trust and rapport needed to work out a solution. I had to "get real" with clients and do it quickly, but I had to establish trust first, or the conversation with our potential client would go nowhere.

A real estate mentor of mine at the time recommended

this book by Jerry Vass titled *Soft Selling in a Hard World*. I loved it, and I think it's worth the read for anyone who wants to remain ethical, moral, and compassionate in the world of sales. I read it in hardcopy, highlighted in it, and made lots of notes in the margins. I still keep it on my bookshelf for reference.

A personal story about actively listening related to aging in place is with my own mother. I have brought my children on many visits to their grandparents' home in the last couple years. Each evening after the children are in bed, my parents and I have our own time to talk as adults. We talk about parenting, work, business, the news, and politics. We also discuss their health, how they are doing, and questions about their house and design ideas, since their son is an architect.

Earlier, while I'd been studying architecture in college, my mother liked to bounce ideas off me about possible renovations in their home. I'd sketch out some thoughts and measurements on paper to show her design solutions in concept.

On one of our recent family visits to my parents' home, I found that my mother had in hand some fairly complete drawings for a master bathroom remodeling project she'd been wanting to do for quite a while. The drawings were beautiful, done in multiple 3-D views and full color. The creator of those drawings was a design company that offers kitchen and bath remodeling design and is also a showroom that sells cabinetry and other products in the Portland, Oregon, area.

As you may know already, the cabinet company can offer to do this high quality drawing in-house and "for free." They'll make plenty of money on the high-priced cabinetry sale and installation in that new kitchen or bathroom they offered those drawings for. So it is a sexy teaser and a "lost leader" of sorts (from a marketing and advertising perspective) that can "hook" the client to an attractive image of a potential "after" look in the space they are considering remodeling. Apparently this tactic works, based on how far down the road my mother was with their company in the design process before I noticed.

As an architect and a CAPS Certified Aging-In-Place Specialist, I was shocked when I looked at the actual bathroom design for a 62-year-old baby boomer couple. There were a multitude of items that did not even remotely consider the *future needs* of my parents! So much was missing in the design as it relates to them personally.

It's funny what happens when good designers ask the right questions—and ask enough questions to get to the *real truth* of the matter. I knew, from talking to my mother, that she pushes off the toilet paper holder to help get up off the water closet (toilet, in layman's terms). I cringed at the thought, as that's exactly the type of makeshift solution that is *an accident and a fall waiting to happen* for my mother, who suffers from severe osteoarthritis.

The standard toilet paper holder is *not* a grab bar. The typical toilet paper holder is held in the drywall (not even lagged into studs behind the wall) by only two small screws and a tiny hidden set screw on each side for the post cover plates. This fixture isn't designed or approved for *any* amount of pressure or weight to be applied to it. There are now designs of toilet paper holders that *do* double as a grab bar and assistive device—when installed correctly, of course. There are towel bars now that do this as well. But neither my mother's existing toilet paper holder fixture—*nor the one proposed with the remodel*—is one of those devices capable of being assistive as a grabbing mechanism or weight-bearing handle.

Most accidents happen in "wet rooms" like the bathroom, kitchen, and laundry room. A great many of these accidents are the result of an aging person still trying to make their standard existing home design and conditions work for them—without the proper modifications. Other accidents are caused when a family member or other caregiver tries to help someone with their ADLs (activities of daily living) in an *unmodified home setting* that doesn't meet the changing needs of the client.

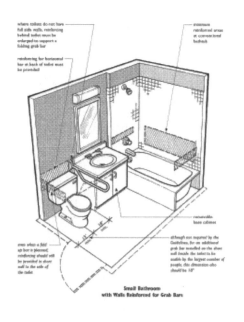

Small Bathroom with Walls Reinforced for Grab Bars

After seeing Mom's drawings, I simply asked her if I might add some edits for her safety that would give me some peace of mind. If she would allow me five minutes and a red pen to put a few notes on the drawings, I could suggest a few changes that she should ask for. Thankfully she let me do it. Her agreement was based on the fact that I had taken time, over the previous two years, to build that trust and rapport with her in such a way that she considered me as someone on her list of trusted advisers.

The mark-ups that I made to their drawings were to put blocking behind the walls in all the locations where a future grab bar might be useful and installed at a later date. That way, when my "I-told-you-so moment" finally came, I wouldn't need to say that to my parents. But more importantly, they wouldn't later have to tear out their brand-new floor to ceiling custom tile shower and the walls around the toilet to install products that will allow them to remain in their own home. There were other things I'd have done differently with the cabinetry as well, but I knew how much I could push the issue at the time, and that would have been too far. I did also edit the entry door, which was a two feet six inch wide in-swinging door. I drew a wider opening at three feet zero inches and specified that it should swing outward into the bedroom. That way the open door wouldn't compromise the interior areas of the bathroom floor, allowing for future mobility with assistive devices such as a walker or wheelchair. I made a couple other notes "for consideration," some of which my folks opted out of at the time of the remodel. But those items are less expensive to come back and fix later, so I decided not to push them. Fortunately, I'd gotten the major things I wanted with my red pen and my five minutes alone with the drawings.

I was happy that my mother let me mark up the drawings. It created a peace of mind for me, which was the way I approached the conversation with her. I felt better as her son—and also as an architect, knowing I'd been able to solve a problem that would arise later related to keeping their independence and having their bathroom function properly when the time comes.

There are some other ways you can proactively position yourself to be able to help a parent, spouse, or other loved one in their later years. Without getting into any detail here, I will list a few of them for reference and your own further research. There are situations where becoming the executor of their will or estate, gaining power of attorney, or taking on some other type of decision-making power on their behalf (legal or otherwise) can be quite helpful. This can ensure your ability to get things accomplished in a timely fashion for them, and to ensure that they continue to be cared for and that they are safe and protected.

This topic alone could be an entire book. I've chosen not to address it in any detail here as it's not my area of expertise. An elder law attorney or an attorney who deals with estate law can be a valuable asset and a great team member in considering all the angles and facets of aging in place.

With a sincere desire to help our loved ones, and a

willingness to take that time and make that effort, we can all do this. We can learn to be active listeners and start working toward solutions for the future. We can take care of our loved ones, even through the challenge of their elder years and end-of-life issues. We can do this, together.

Chapter Five:

Planning Ahead is Key to a Successful Outcome

An ounce of prevention is worth a pound of cure.
—Benjamin Franklin

WHO BETTER TO BRING to the table as a quotable leader and inspiration than the great Ben Franklin. His adage is proof that we've been speaking this public message of planning ahead for a very *long time*.

At ADM Architecture, my own firm, we regularly explain to clients that "It takes $1 to move a line in a drawing on paper, but it takes $1000 to move a wall after it's been built and you don't like where it is." Planning in the design phase matters. Working through different ideas and solutions in advance, even if it takes a few more revisions, is money well spent. It costs much less than making mistakes or changes "in the field" during construction. Therefore, our argument for the *value of design and planning* is that we "more than pay for ourselves" by getting it right on paper first—and in *mistakes not made* during construction of the project.

This same idea transfers over to the process and goals of aging in place. The best possible outcomes emerge from careful and thoughtful collaboration and planning in the design phase. We plan ahead, putting as much effort into *future solutions thinking* as possible—prior to the acute occurrence that will eventually take place in an older person's life. Without planning, that acute occurrence will immediate place us, literally in an instant, from the opportunity of "planning our future" to the least desirable position of panic and reaction. The latter option is drenched in the desperate need for quick decisions, now forced upon us in the midst of the emotionally overwhelming situation we are in "after the fact" of an acute occurrence (such as a fall or illness) that results in hospitalization or surgery for you or a loved one. This scenario is drastically more costly—in every way—than planning in advance.

Right now, in the design phase, is the time where your professional team including a CAPS certified architect can bring the *most value and wisdom* to a successful solution and outcome for you, your family, and your loved ones.

SUCCESS STORY:

I received a call from a woman we'll call Susan who heard about our aging in place residential design through her sister, my son's swim teacher. Thanks to my networking and good relationship with his swim teacher, this woman was inspired to call me. What I loved about the conversation was her approach and attitude. Susan was clear that she wanted to stay in her own home, a unique oval-shaped curvilinear house on Bainbridge Island that her husband had designed, and they had constructed, with their shared dream of how they would live there together. Susan's husband suffered three strokes in the final years of his life, passing away a few years ago. She had been his caregiver during those final years. Susan explained that they had made some accessibility modifications on the surface to help him, and to allow her to better assist help him in bathing. She went on to say, quite matter-of-factly, that she was recently diagnosed with early Parkinson's disease, and that she is experiencing some tremors in her legs and feet.

During my initial site visit, Susan calmly told me her expectations of the disease's progression. She recognized that what worked for her husband design-wise (as accessories and mobility devices in their home) would not work for her personal needs, living alone and with different ailments. I was impressed with Susan's perfect awareness and honesty in grappling with the truth of her situation. She also understood that a successful aging in place solution will be specific to each individual: their stature, height, weight, age, personal issues of mobility and cognition, as well as their personal living arrangement. If I could transfer her understanding and clarity to every person in this country, I would! What a perfect client.

Bainbridge Island Home - Entry Sketch by ADM Architecture

I am fortunate to be working with her now on the redesign of her master bathroom, as well as coordinating access in her walk-in closet. We are editing the front entry stairs so she will be able to enter her home via a ramp that is eloquently tied into the existing stairs, railings, and landscaping along the front of the home. In her living room area, we'll improve the layout so that her favorite chair relates better to the entertainment center location, allowing better TV viewing without the morning glare coming in. Building out a thicker wall at the entertainment center area will also allow us to recess the equipment and reroute or remove the exposed cords and trip hazards that are currently a safety risk. I feel honored and blessed to help such a wonderful client.

Clients like Susan are part of the massive majority of Americans who want to remain in their own homes as they grow older (up to 89 percent as polled by AARP). So I take every opportunity I'm given to speak about aging in place and the challenges that lie ahead for the housing industry. The multi-billion dollar CCRC industry (Continuing Care Retirement Communities) only captures about 5 to 8 percent of the U.S. population, in spite of the millions of dollars they spend on sales, marketing, renovations, and advertising. Why is this the case? We simply don't want to move, and we don't want to *have to* live there. We don't want to concede to the transition any earlier than is truly necessary. I want to be clear here: we are not arguing that "facilities" don't have a place in our continuum of care. They do, and they're an essential option we'll all consider over the course of our family's lives. I'm not arguing *if* we might need to make that move, but rather *when*. What I'm suggesting is that with foresight and planning we can (and would prefer to) *postpone* that transition for many folks for a significant amount of time. We can do that with good planning and design, together.

I educate homeowners, jurisdictions, and the building industry at every chance I get, presenting to local industry associations and civic and philanthropic groups. I also write articles, co-host a radio show, and maintain multiple Web sites for that purpose of educating the public.

I share my thoughts, resources, and feedback on information that's timely and topical to the industry via a multitude of social media outlets such as LinkedIn, Twitter, and Facebook. These newer social platforms allow easy access to our resources at two different sites. ADM Architecture (at www.ADM-architecture.com) offers general architectural and commercial developer information as well as information on the residential side of our firm that is specifically aligned with baby boomers, their families and caregivers. The majority of this residential information is shared at www.EmpoweringTheMatureMind.com through blogging, white papers, podcasts, and webinars. Here you will also find our online newsletter, which you can sign up to receive.

I also author contributions to other online media publications and national print literature.

I have interviewed experts and been interviewed by thought leaders in the industry from across the nation. In August 2012 I began co-hosting a radio show in Seattle called "Encore Living" that is now on the Internet at www. BlogTalk Radio.com/EncoreLiving. I recently delivered one of our most popular presentations in Chicago (in the spring of 2013) at the "Aging In America" conference put on by the American Society on Aging. The four-day event was attended by thousands of people, including other professionals, national thought leaders, and industry experts. Some people who attend my presentations experience a flurry of mixed emotions afterwards. They are brought into an awareness of the possibilities of their future, possibilities of illness, mortality, and issues we would rather avoid. Instead of saying "I wish I'd known," the listener has to admit, "well, now I do." Instead of seeing these issues *in hindsight* with 20/20 vision when it's too late, you now have an opportunity to be proactive for your own sake and the sake of people you love.

So what can planning ahead do for you?

- Save your hard-earned money.

- Save your lifestyle in your home.

- Extend your finances during retirement.

- Extend your happiness, longevity, and safety at home.

- Save your independence, your dignity, and your right to choose your housing situation.

Save Your Hard Earned Money:

I've written a white paper for the financial planning and retirement asset management industries titled "There's $500,000 Hiding in Your Home." I'll share the gist of it with you. My paper compares the average cost of two different elder living situations for a ten- to fifteen-year duration. Remodeling your home for aging in place is the first scenario. Moving to a unit in an assisted-living or nursing home type facility is the second scenario. Comparing the cost of living in a CCRC facility, I show how remodeling your home (and the associated costs) would actually *save you approximately $32,000+ per year,* even when you include part time in home care at 20 hours per week.

Here's the aging in place example I used, and I intentionally showed the price of a *major* remodeling project to prove my point. Let's assume that you, a typical baby boomer with a decent credit score and a fair amount of equity in your home, took out a loan against your house to do a $150,000 remodeling project to transform all the issues and obstacles of your current home into the ideal conditions of your "forever home." At that price point, we are including things like a kitchen remodel for better layout and appliances/fixtures, a master bath remodel, retrofitting your third or fourth bedroom and part of the family room downstairs to include an elevator, and modifications to your master bedroom and bathroom for Universal Design components—all for a successful aging in place outcome in consideration of a future mobility assistance device like a walker or a wheelchair. Or we could design a layout that is specific to an ailment that's common in your family history, let's say ALS or Parkinson's.

A "Home Equity Line of Credit" (HELOC) or second mortgage, using round numbers for simplicity at a good 5 percent interest rate (due to your credit score and loan-to-value ratio) would equate to a monthly payment on the new loan of just $750 per month.

Compare that to the average rate per month for a room in an assisted-living facility. The national average for a unit (room) in an assisted-living or nursing home facility (based on 2010 statistical numbers we found in researching the topic) come out to $3,000 to $6,000 per month, depending on the rating and location of the facility and the level of care you require. (https://www.metlife.com/mmi/research/2011-market-survey-long-term-care-costs.html#findings)

Knowing that health care is a part of the cost of the facility setting, I wanted to make the comparison between these two options more realistic during the 10 to 15 years that we feel people would prefer, and likely can, stay in their own home longer. Therefore, I added the cost considerations of the potential care you may need during your extended stay in your own home. At 20 hours per week, an in home care agency can provide assistance with the ADL's (Activities of Daily Living) in and around your home if and when any of your abilities or needs begin to change. That service is available at a national average rate of $19 to $21 per hour and is accounted for in this comparison.

If we add the annual cost of a second loan on your home that allows you to remodel it to stay there, plus the in home assistance you may need to stay there (at 20 hours per week), the annual total is approximately ***$33,600 less*** than the cost of a live-in facility!

Extend that total out for 10 to 15 years and there's the amount I reference in the title of that white paper: *over $500,000 in savings* in your retirement years. The research and findings were astounding when I put this information together, and it confirmed for me that we *can* help our older Americans to do exactly what they *want* to do, which is to *stay in their own community, in their own home* with their memories, friends, pet(s), and their garden.

Again, I'm using simple math and round numbers to quickly show you this. Everyone's situation and finances will be different, which is a point I'll get to in more detail in the next chapter about having a professional team of advocates in your corner for the best AIP outcome possible.

Save Your Lifestyle in Your Own Home:

This is where you live and where you want to continue to live. Things are familiar, and you are comfortable and at ease with your surroundings. You are allowed to have

your pet here. You are allowed to make your own schedule here, including when and where you go during the
day, when you'll eat and what you'll have for your meals.
It's where you decide who you see and when you want to
see them. It's "home base" for your comforts in life. It's
the place you can depart from for your retirement trav-
els, pleasure, and visiting family—and know it will be just
the way you left it when you return. It's where you feel in
control of your lifestyle, and that's an important piece of
your vitality and happiness.

Extend Your Finances During Retirement:

For many of you, your last third of life transitions you
into more of a fixed income than you may have been used
to in the latter years of your professional career. This
requires planning for your comfort and examining your
financial lifestyle level in light of these potentially new
financial parameters. Aging in place can be, as pointed
out mathematically in item #1 above, a potentially huge
factor in this equation, and in your financial success and
longevity in retirement. There are many ways to look at
extending your finances in retirement, and we recommend having a financial planner as a part of your trusted
adviser team for any solution—aging in place included.

Extend Your Happiness, Longevity, and Safety at Home:

Home is where you are happiest. It's what you know. It's where you have made a multitude of memories with your family and friends, and it's where all of your own things are, and you know where they are located. Being at home is where your routine is based, and it is comfortable. Our research has even run across polls that suggest that on average, being a homeowner and staying in your own home can *add* an average of *seven years* to your life. So home can be a crucial component in your longevity, and the opportunity to increase it. Since we as a nation have added an additional 30 or so years to our lives in the last century, it's reasonable that we should, individually, think about how to increase our personal longevity as well.

This may be one of the blessings that occurs when a professional team of advisers can create with you the opportunities to make your home work better and be safer for you as you stay home longer. My own grandfather, at age 93, is currently working on a project in his backyard to remove some overbearing bamboo with a root system which has compromised some of the adjacent yard. He had been a career farmer who sold his own 26 acres of Christmas trees and flowers, and he is acutely aware of the need to resolve this issue of the bamboo's rampant rooting system. Grandpa spent the last few months working with landscaping contractors and nursery owners at his home, getting advice and working alongside them to get rid of the bamboo, rework the soils, and prepare the area for his new choice: a line of blueberry bushes along the backyard fence.

This is a perfect example of how home-ownership can be good for your longevity. Owning a home can inspire and even force you at times into the "use it or lose it" part of exercising both your body and mind related to problem solving things that occur with your home. When you live in a facility setting, you don't have to find someone to mow your lawn. You don't have to ask around to find a plumber, contact him, set up an appointment, meet with him, and discuss the issues about your sink in order to come to a conclusion. You don't have to cook. You don't have to do much of anything if you don't want to; it can all be a part of the facility plan that you choose for included services when you move in. In that vein of "use it or lose it," it can be detrimental for some people to give up all the things that used to exercise their brain and body. This can be a potentially risky proposition to their longevity plan.

Safety is a big key to ensuring that aging in your own home is a smart and successful housing solution choice. There are many great products available now for your home that didn't exist 20 years ago, and some of them are designed to help maintain your ability to maneuver safely within the house and go about your daily life, even as your mobility may decrease over time. I'm speaking about way more than just a grab bar in your shower, that's for sure!

Flooring materials, lighting fixtures, smart appliances, levered door handles and faucets that work just by touching them, walk-in tubs, ramps, lifts, residential elevators, hoist systems for the bedroom and bathing area, and a multitude of other products are coming into the marketplace to meet aging in place needs. There are more new products, and improvements to existing products, coming onto the market place all the time!

Progress in this area will continue to be made for many years ahead as industries pay attention to baby boomers and their housing and purchasing preferences. It is how all of these products *go together*, and are specifically chosen and installed to meet each client's specific needs, which requires a professional architect or certified home designer. And this expert needs specialized knowledge of the clientele in these market sectors: that's *you* and your family, parents, and loved ones. Successful aging in place relies on good design and implementation of the products and systems that are made to increase our safely (and thereby our longevity) in our own home. Client-driven design and correct implementation is how you can stay home—safer, longer, happier, and healthier.

Save your independence, your dignity, and your right to choose your housing situation:

The previous four points all feed into this final point. Being safe at home through good design allows you to stay there and stay independent. Staying independent allows you to keep your dignity. Remaining in control of your own lifestyle and maintaining it on your own terms is empowering and critical to your mental health as well. You can stay where you choose to live and keep the life you want without burdening your family members, children, or others, to meet your daily needs and maintain your daily routine. Even if down the road you may need assistance with driving, cooking, or other similar tasks, *having the right to choose where you live* is what you want for yourself. I want that for you as well, and it's a valiant and intimately personal goal that is valid to pursue and achieve.

And what if you *don't* plan ahead?

An accident or illness can alter the direction of your life, instantly.

Your life decisions can start being made by others in the blink of any eye, and for the remainder of your life.

You can lose your independence, your dignity, and your ability to fulfill your own wants, needs, wishes and rights—where, when, and how you want.

You can become a burden on others whom you love.

You can drain your finances before your retirement years are over, and possibly devastate the financial futures of your family, friends, and loved ones.

So in reality, the choices and consequences go back to Mr. Franklin again:

"By failing to prepare, you are preparing to fail."
—Benjamin Franklin

This isn't what we want for anyone.

The decisions regarding our housing situation and our medical care (where we'll live and how our care will be delivered and administered to us), will likely be the two biggest financial (and emotional) decisions that factor into the success of our longevity outcome; that includes the factor of our retirement funds as well. If we don't do this critical part proactively, an accident could decide everything for us. And with that unexpected event, all the other choices we would have liked to have the freedom to make in our "golden years" of retirement will be swept away with it.

But we can take charge. Even though none of us can predict the future, none of us need to be victims of circumstance in our later years. Together, we can create positive outcomes by being empowered, taking responsibility, and making things happen. Let's be in charge of our future!

Chapter Six:

Hiring a Professional Team is Critical to Your Success

"Happiness is not something you postpone for the future; it is something you design for the present."
—Jim Rohn

THERE IS A TENDENCY to think of the architecture industry as a superfluous expenditure, a luxury item. The down economy as of 2007 hasn't helped that perception, nor has it helped architects' ability to make a living at their chosen profession in the design and building industries. Add to that all of the technology advances, and we've practically come back full circle to the era where you could buy a house out of the Sears Roebuck catalog. We now have access via the Internet to thousands of these pre-designed "spec" (speculative) houses. All these factors have made it a challenge to succeed as a residential architect, and to share the message of aging in place.

These pre-designed speculative units you can see on

the Internet are the types of houses that have filled suburbia, where you only know which house is yours by what
side of the yard the driveway and the one tree are on,
along with the address number and the color of the front
door. Other than those very minor façade alterations and
"mirror image" flip-flopped floor plans, it all seems to
look basically the same.

As an architect, I find this to be unfortunate. The first
home I purchased was like this, and the design solutions
continued to be downright frustrating. The only design
consideration by the builder and developer of these massive expanses of tract homes is how to maximize the
heated livable (and sellable) square footage inside the
home on that postage stamp sized lot. And to maximize
the total number of lots created, the developer minimized
setbacks from every property line, therefore practically
obliterating usable outside space in the yard.

I have worked as a designer for both residential builders and larger scale multi-family developers who were
so focused on their business model priorities that they
seemed to have lost sense of the "you" who would inhabit
their buildings. They don't think about *you*; they are
focused on their business model priorities. I've designed
custom infill housing in desirable areas of Seattle for a
builder, where at his request (and per his own profitability modeling information related to the market and
buyer demographic of that desirable neighborhood),
we've gotten more house square footage inside than
there is lot square footage total. It's gross, in my honest

opinion. Massive houses of 4,800 square feet cast shadows most of the day on the adjacent house 10 feet away. Due to 5-foot side yard property line setbacks, and with 2-foot roof overhangs that cut into that setback, you have 28- to 30-foot-tall homes with gutters that are only 6 *feet apart!* Does any of this sound like something *you* would intentionally do if you were designing your own custom home? I didn't think so, and that's our point. Speculative builder houses are *not* designed *for you,* but for that right-handed, fully able-bodied, statistically average person (that very few of us are). But now we have the option of designing living spaces that are customized based on your own personal needs and desires.

Now, aside from the complete lack of character and modulation in the façade of these homes, and the miniscule exterior spaces on each property in this type of neighborhood, there is a bigger issue at hand. All across the housing industry, we have *failed to invest any foresight or planning to meet the changing needs of our population.* And these needs are about to hit us head-on. These builder-designed homes don't consider aging in place on either the inside or the outside of these homes. Interior spaces (outside of the popular "great room" living room, dining room, and kitchen area) are consistently the minimum that they can be, to fit as many bedrooms and as many full or partial bathrooms into the maximized "box," I mean house, size on the tiny lot. Subsequently, these decisions have been driven by the "stats that sell" on the real estate market—*in the past.*

The result for the boomer buyer these days—and in the next 20 to 30 years—is that there is no real room to make modifications under the current bedroom/bathroom count that might accommodate the changing needs of the next three to four buyers of this home during the Silver Tsunami years ahead. Then on the outside, the pathway from our cars into our houses takes no consideration of how our mobility might change in the second half of our lives. Speculative houses are fairly ignorant to the topography of our building sites, so problems in elevation are solved—by default—with stairs. There is no thoughtfulness in site location for the home, and no grading of the land to make access easier for all people.

Here's a perfect interiors example. I addressed this photo from my first home in a blog titled "Speculative—The Impersonal and Short-Sighted House." Look at this photo. What's wrong with it? The answer is simple, but the premise is much deeper and more disturbing.

The drawer in the bathroom cannot open all the way when the in-swinging door to the bathroom is fully opened. None of the drawers in this cabinet would work properly with this bathroom door open. This is one of only two drawers for storage in the sink cabinet. The top drawer face is actually false because they also made the mistake of where the sink plumbing is located in the wall, which won't allow for the top drawer to function. So it had to be taken out and a "false front" installed. For a homeowner, this is annoying. To an architect, this reveals a disturbing and frustrating lack of consideration for any actual user of the home. This is spec building at its best, I'd say—facetiously of course! I can solve some issues and challenges like these that you may face in your own spec home so that you can make better and safer use of your home and can successfully age in place. Some solutions are simple and low cost, while others take more creativity and expense to resolve.

As a licensed architect and CAPS Certified Aging-in-Place Specialist, I'm focused on the future of housing in the United States related to the explosion in the aging baby boomer and less-able populations. How can we create housing appropriate to serve these needs? This issue is staring us dead in the face. This is the SILVER TSUNAMI of the next 2 decades. We either start paddling together, and *fast*, or we drown as professionals for "missing the boat."

I'm concerned by the overall thoughtlessness in design that has become painfully prevalent in the majority of the "speculative" housing stock products, now that we are looking at a new demographic of longevity. Most builders have become—either by personal agenda or by simple financial calculations that required cutting of soft costs—their own "self-professed designers." They continue to build what they know best, the way they've done it for decades.

You don't have to be a licensed architect to design a house, as long as a structural engineer stamps the drawings for the "will it stand up" and "will it handle the local wind and snow loads" factors of building design. But it's high time for us to relinquish the "speculative" housing model altogether, and to build housing stock adaptable to many needs. It's high time—among general contractors, builders, and architects—for *serious teamwork that centers around aging in place considerations*. This requires more professional collaboration and expertise than we've needed in the past.

I believe that the wider the inclusion of critical expertise and professionals who collaborate for a client's needs and desires, the better the outcome—for those clients, and for our society at large. The potential for success is multiplied by bringing together the architect, builder, and even the occupational therapist, financial planner, and others who qualify as part of your own team of trusted advisers.

So what is the risk of "thoughtless and short-sighted design"? Let me start by saying that I know and work with many very talented general contractors (GCs) who bring amazing insight and intellectual value to the design team and to the client. That's not the issue here. This issue is about where the country is going and what we—the building industry as a whole—are not paying attention to. I feel that new construction can do a much better job of "looking forward" and, during the initial construction of new homes, planning for future modifications to suit the needs of any potential buyer or occupant.

The general public has the perception that the architect's job is to create aesthetic "beauty" for the exterior and interior design of a home. However, an architect does much more than this. Here is a short, basic (and very partial) quick-list, showing some additional and highly valuable things that an architect does during the design and creation of a specific home for a specific client:

1. Programming: Meeting the client multiple times to learn about them specifically, including (just to name a few):

    - How they function in their home

    - What they do and don't like about their existing accommodations

    - How they use each space in their daily lives

    - If they entertain, how and when they house guests and how many people / how many times per year

    - What vehicles they drive

- How many children they have, how often those children are home

- What their hobbies are, and what spaces accommodate those hobbies

2. Design: Meeting the client multiple times to work though the sizes, locations, and relationships (adjacencies) of each space based on the specific client's programming goals. This is done directly with the client at least two or three times (minimum) as the design solutions are created. Each design phase evolves and expands from initially just floor plan layouts of each floor, into the exterior elevations, building and wall construction sections, and then additional design drawings and details related to the interior elevations in critical areas such as the kitchen and bathrooms, etc. Design can also include specific extra drawings depending on the level of involvement the architect is hired for, such as lighting plans, power and data plans, room finish plans and schedules, door and window types and schedules, and even including fixture schedules for appliances, lighting, and hardware, among others.

3. Permitting: Leading or helping the client with submittal of the appropriate forms, documents, and drawings.

4. Codes: The IRC (International Residential Code) and compliance with those codes in creation of the

documents and drawings, along with all the local jurisdictional requirements related to your specific property parcel, zoning code, setbacks, site restrictions, height limits, allowable structure types, etc.

I've taken on numerous clients who have come to my architecture firm *after* trying to avoid using a design professional. They had been unsuccessful at navigating the use of "Internet drawings" they had purchased, when trying to submit it for approval specific to their own personal property parcel, site, and in their local jurisdiction.

5. Advocacy in Construction Observation/Administration: Acting as the owner's representative and advocate for the "checks and balances" that are important in the client relationship with the general contractor during the course of construction. For example, the architect can manage the payment schedule from client to GC based on site visits and weekly meetings during construction wherein the architect would verify milestones of completion, review any change orders created by the contractor, and provide confirmation of the work being completed on site meeting the specifications and design intent of the drawings prior to payment.

We explain to our clients (while using our two index fingers and two thumbs to make a triangle) that a good team has a triangle relationship that keeps it in balance—in this case, among the client, contractor, and architect.

Pulling my thumbs apart, I say, "If you take one of the three points—the architect—away," now showing only my two index fingers joined horizontally at their tips, "then you're left with only two parties (the client and the general contractor) and the resulting 'he said, she said' finger-pointing relationship." That's not what I want for my clients.

I was asked by a CAPS Occupational Therapist to come assess a house for an early Parkinson's patient in one of our local neighborhoods in Seattle. In my two-hour professional site consultation, I was able to measure, sketch, and resolve a design solution for his two wheelchairs to better maneuver from the bedroom, down the hall, and into the (also reconfigured) kitchen and bathroom. He would now be able to maneuver appropriately to utilize a new sink with under-counter clearance, a new roll-in shower, and a more appropriate water closet (toilet) fixture. This is the value that a CAPS designer brings to the table. For me, that experience and training is in addition to 8 years of full time schooling and field architecture firm work experience, followed then by the 9 tests (totaling 36 hours of exams) that it takes to become a licensed architect in my state.

As I said before, I have great contractors whom I work with every day. These people are extremely knowledgeable and capable, bringing expertise and experience to the client and to the design/construction table that I do not have. Hence, we need to and should value each other. What

I *do* worry about is the "Mr. Fix-It" guy who likely oblivious to, or at best, under-educated about, aging in place issues. This person may say, "Sure, I can install a grab bar; what do you need an architect for?" This is what I find dangerous to the client, and frustrating to my profession. Hopefully, now you have some idea of the value that only a professional designer can bring to your design team and to your successful aging in place solution. This is far beyond what your contractor, developer, handyman, or builder can do alone.

Do you remember, from chapter two, who the average home and our community environment is designed for? The "basic speculative design" of most man-made spaces around us is created for: a right-handed, able-bodied adult, of average height and weight, with full mobility range and strength, perfect eyesight, perfect hearing, and the ability to communicate verbally with another human being. Is that you? If you are lucky enough that it is today, will this still be you in 10, 20, or 30 years? It's high time for a paradigm shift.

General contractors are an invaluable part of the design and construction team. Architects and designers know this, and the work we get in our firms goes on to them and keeps them employed as they are needed to build what we design. Unfortunately there are some contractors (or more often builder/developers) who don't feel that's a two-way street in terms of the value an architect brings to the design and construction team, especially in the residential realm.

As I pointed out previously, we are back to a "catalog house plan" society with the invention of the Internet, where selecting a home is like picking from a very abbreviated catalog that offers a minimal amount of choice and variation in what's available. My biggest concern is that this results in homes that are not easily "adaptable." *Good design from the beginning* proves to be the best scenario for adaptability—to later accommodate the changing housing needs that arise for each individual.

The typical builder has been doing the same thing for 30+ years and has his "tried and true" way of doing things. He has his spreadsheet way of thinking about solutions and options, he's done his own style of math, and he knows how to deliver to his customer the best product for the price—*based on the old model.* As shrewd businessmen, most builders aren't interested in anything that would alter their bottom line by being "more expensive" in any way. If you suggest something that increases their costs or reduces their profits, very few are open to listen—regardless of the market need, forward thinking, future forecasting, or society betterment that could result. When planned from *inception,* however, the end result *does not* have to cost more.

When we consider planning ahead versus modifying later, it's easy to see that good design from the beginning of the project can create a home that's easily adaptable for future alterations (and considerations of the changing buyer). I speak to industry associations on this topic as well, and hope that the B2B (business to business) educational efforts will help create *new housing stock* in the U.S.: homes that are *adaptable* and designed with the consideration that *anyone would be able to get to, enter, and use* this house, regardless of their level of physical ability or the potential use of any mobility devices. This "adaptable home" design, planning for the future from the very inception of the original construction, would go a long way toward successful aging in place for these next 30 years of housing needs, here in the United States and beyond.

Some general contractors may offer to make aging in place alterations to a client's home without recommending the inclusion of a professional designer. Perhaps it's a good time for me to stand up for my industry as a professional licensed and adequately credentialed designer, and help set the record straight about *why you do need an architect*—especially one who understands this specific client's needs and project type as a CAPS Certified Aging-in-Place Specialist.

Not to throw anyone under the bus, but just to prove a point, I have a few questions for that "non-CAPS certified" general contractor about you, their prospective client for a residential remodeling or new construction project.

Mr/s. General Contractor:

1) Do you know what the client's occupational therapist, physical therapist, or geriatric care manager recommends? Which grab bar is going to work best for this client? What possible options are there? What are the specifications on that particular mobility device? At what height should it be installed specifically for this client? At what angle? What mobility issues is it supporting for this client? What range of motion does this client have in this activity, position orientation, and location?

2) Do you know the specifications on the client's wheelchair, walker, or other mobility devices if she has one? What's the turning radius? Do you know of other options that may suit the client better than her current device? If she doesn't have an occupational or physical therapist, do you have readily available professional recommen-dations for who could help with OT/PT (occupa-tional or physical therapy) input? Do you know where to send the client and her family members to look at other mobility device options?

3) Do you know not only what the client's budget is for the potential construction project work at the house, but also how that budget/cost ties into their overall plan for their (likely fixed income) funds in retirement? Have you discussed with the client how their monthly cash flow and expenses would be affected by proceeding with this home project?

Do you know how the project you are proposing will affect the client's ability to pay for in home care after the remodel? Are you aware and clear about the client's ability to make a financing payment based on the income distributions that their investments are paying out monthly/annually?

4) Do you know how to address and advise the client on different ways they can fund the project, who they can trust to finance an aging in place remodel, and what a "reverse mortgage" is? Who might the client talk with to see if it might make sense for their situation? After learning about this client's conditions, wants, and needs, if it appears that staying at home is not the best answer for their situation, do you have the ability to discuss "other housing solutions" with them? Suppose this client wishes to consider other housing options as well, in order to compare them to remodeling their own home for aging in place. Do you know where in their area to send this client to look at other housing options?

5) Do you know all the aspects of a quality aging in place experience? Do you understand how daylight affects the client's psychological health? Do you know that white surfaces can cause vertigo in Alzheimer's clients? Do you understand how various factors could potentially "make or break" this client's happiness and functional use of their remodel? I'm speaking about colors, transitions, lighting, fixture locations, heights, floor plan layout, cabinet elevations & upgrades, appliance selections, installation heights and locations—as they relate to the specific client.

I'm just offering up a couple of questions for that general contractor who is considering getting you to work with him—without including me. These are the types of questions I would ask, discuss, and coordinate with my own clients. These are just a few examples of the items I would want to address with you and for you, to ensure that together as a team, you and I create a successful aging in place design solution that is driven by your actual individualized and personal situation, your wants, needs, fears, and desires.

The bottom line: Does the typical general contractor know what our aging in place client's *goals* are?   Or their *limitations*? Their *concerns*? Remember, the truth is always "three levels deep..." Is this typical contractor trained to ask the questions that will uncover the real answers?

*I am an aging in place **coach** in all reality, a professional concierge of sorts. Maybe you could even call me an "AIP Quarterback."* I am *one valuable team member* among a variety of professionals who, together, form an All-Star team of advisers for helping a client to stay in their home. Our clients in this field and demographic want respect, trust, value, and a complete "turnkey" solution. These clients appreciate our collaborative efforts where all team members are honest, ethical, and communicate well with each other.

So how do you choose a good architect or appropriately credentialed home designer?

We recommend the following criteria:

- 8-10 or more years in the industry of residential and/or multi-family housing design.

- Licensing that solidifies their credibility to do housing design projects. This could include: licensed architect (at the highest end) or other certified home designer credentials (titles and organizations may vary by region and state).

- Additional experience, training, and coursework related to designing for the specifics of older populations. This could include: CAPS ("Certified Aging-in-Place Specialist" through NAHB), CSA (Ceritifed Senior Advisor), and UD (Universal Design Certification), among other similar courses and certifications.

- Reference/Referrals: Ask to contact 2 or 3 of their clients (preferably from the past 1-3 years) who would be willing to share their experience of working with that person or firm.

- People Skills: Trust your instincts on this one. Look for good listening, comprehension, and clear articulation. Look for sincerity and someone with the ability to keep your best interests in mind from the onset of your project through its completion.

Speaking only for ourselves as a licensed architecture design firm, we personally would hope that our clients would consider us as their best design team member based on these credentials:

1. I have the training, the National Association of Home Builders' national accreditation of being a CAPS Certified Aging-In-Place Specialist. My firm has the niche industry and business model homework established, and it is a continually ongoing effort. We have the professional relationships established through almost two decades in the fields of architecture and real estate investing. We have the professional networking connections across Washington State, growing quickly toward a nationwide database of connections and relationships in this specific field and niche industry.

2. Through ongoing homework, we have a clear understanding of the other industries that are required to
interface with this client and their "staying at home"
solution. I can refer my clients to all the potential
"team members" they may need in their area for
completing that dream of aging in place. This includes (but is not limited to) CAPS certified general
contractors, CAPS certified interior designers, CAPS
certified occupational therapists, physical therapists,
financial planners, retirement asset managers, reverse mortgage specialists, and elder law attorneys.

3. I have an architectural license with 17+ years of experience in the field. I completed the required eight
years of combined college level architecture education
via schooling and the subsequent associated ap-
prentice work under a licensed architect in a firm. I
completed the preparation and studies required to sit
for the 9 tests (totaling 36 *hours* of exams) to become
a licensed architect in our state.

4. I have been a part of designing over one million
square feet of "ADA Accessible" commercial buildings—including the design, permitting, and construction of shell & core office buildings, retail
spaces, interior tenant improvements, warehouses,

auto dealerships, and research and development facilities. We've worked in all construction materials including steel, concrete, CMU, stucco, and wood, among others. We've done site planning for millions of square feet of public buildings, which includes working with civil engineers for layout of parking, sidewalks, egress into and out of buildings, as well as accessible restrooms and commercial elevators within these building types. This is a small representative summary of my own professional background.

5. I am well versed and experienced as a residential architect and real estate investor. I bought 18 houses in a 24-month period during the last five to seven years. I have renovated and flipped houses for retail sale, held rental homes, and been a landlord for multiple homes, as well as executed "lease options" (rent-to-own programs). At some points, we were buying a home, remodeling two homes, and selling or renting a home—all simultaneously. Therefore, I fully understand discussions about "recouping remodeling costs" and the "resale" concerns of our clients. I have a solid understanding of real estate contracts related to purchase and sale, and can evaluate investment and spending decisions in light of the client's return on investment, if that is of concern in the remodel for aging in place. I am also familiar with the fair market value and valuation approach of homes in different areas.

Most importantly, as a result of all this train-ing and experience, I can listen and empathize with the emotional challenges that face the client throughout this process in relation to spending money on their home.

So, in my own humble yet educated opinion, *"I can install a grab bar"* **just isn't enough for our clients.**

Chapter Seven:

Planning for a Successful Living Environment in Your Own Community: What Does That Look Like Now?

"Nobody wants to be alone. Nobody wants to depend on others. And NOBODY EVER wants to be STORED AWAY. So I don't understand, as an Architect, why we have 17,000 Nursing Homes in this country, which are designed and built to do EXACTLY THAT."
—Matthias Hollwich

AS WE LOOK TOWARD the next couple of decades ahead here and in other developed countries, our challenge is the same. We are getting older, and we are living longer. We can't deny it or ignore it, and we must embrace and plan for it if we want the journey to be a successful one. Proactive planning is the key. Ignorance and avoidance will ensure failure.

This is a chance for us all (as multiple industries look for ways to address the challenges and opportunities of the Silver Tsunami), to get very serious about thinking "outside the box." The 80+ year old population is the fastest growing sector of our U.S. demographic. We've never experienced this in our history. So let's think about ways to get beyond our usual thinking, to act differently, and to be a part of the solution!

I see the down economy as an opportunity to experiment, challenge the "norms" with new ideas, and propose things that just might solve multiple current problems that don't yet have solutions.

Design Solutions for Aging in Place: The Big Picture

For those of you who are truly intrigued by the wave of aging in place for our future, I recommend that you block out the time to watch a YouTube video titled **"Designing Homes and Neighborhoods for an Aging Population: Design Solutions for Aging in Place" by the Milken Institute.** This video in its entirety is 1 hour and 27 minutes long, and provides in-depth knowledge and background information on what's happening in our industry and the discussions that are taking place across the nation. It includes some great insight as to what drives our opinions and ideas here.

Designing Homes and Neighborhoods for an Aging
Population: Design Solutions for Aging in Place

Ellen Dunham-Jones, Georgia Institute of Technology,

Matthias Hollwich, Hollwich Kushner Architects (HWKN)

Christine Nocar, National Church Residences

Moderator: Christopher Leinberger, senior fellow, Brookings Institution

The single family housing being built today is not what
we will need in the decades ahead. Current land use and
zoning codes will trap us in our homes when we give up
our car keys. Let me elaborate on this point for a moment.

Suburban sprawl is basically *over*, in our opinion—at
least at some level that's important enough to explore
here. Understanding just how the integration of skate-
boarders and walkers can live together is the *future,*
also known as "multi-generational housing." Here's the
general lowdown on where the opportunities lie if we are
to solve this problem and make our "new reality" for the
decades ahead.

1) For the last 60 years we've requested suburban sprawl
and we have created drive-able communities. Now,
"Millennials" (the "kids" that came after "Gen X") are
swinging the pendulum back and asking for *less* cars
(tired of traffic early in their careers I guess) and more
walk-able communities. Millennials make up only a
slightly smaller portion of the population than baby
boomers, and together, the two sectors are *over half*
of the U.S. population. Oh, and guess what? Now that

the baby boomers are retiring, and soon won't be driving as much, they are asking for the *same thing*. More *urban* housing solutions. Suburban lifestyle is coming to an end. "Gentrification" is the next generation, and it requires affordable housing solutions, not just the "drive until you qualify" (for a nursing home) approach.

2) Attributes of a young family's suburban single family home that worked then, don't work now. Now they are obstacles to aging in place. Large lot privacy of yesteryear now equates to maintenance issues and a potential perception of isolation. The single-use zoning and school-based centers around housing popular in the past are fading in comparison to the daily needs and access to health care we need now. The desire to drive back then results in neighborhoods that are not truly walk-able now in the ways we need them to be. Therefore, there is a *huge opportunity* to link the needs of aging populations with the expired, vacant, dilapidated, and out of date suburban commercial properties that are currently depreciating neighborhoods and their surroundings. Creative ideas implemented in unlikely properties can be solutions!

Mistakes in housing development design are being made *right now*. A midsized jurisdiction in western Washington is looking at "Older American" housing solutions and "cottage housing," yet the solutions they are coming up with are to create residential communities *outside* of town, on a *hill*, and with a housing model style that is *"split-level." What?!* I was floored to hear this, and I'm trying to get in touch with them before they pursue this huge error in judgment.

Today your developers and builders are still building something that you and I would readily admit we'd never want to live in as we look down the road together with proactive planning in mind. And yet builders are still designing homes that are hazardous and dangerous (two-story, with skinny halls and narrow doors) in relation to what all of us will need as we age... And it's *not that far away.* They are still designing neighborhood solutions and creating urban planning that will *trap you* the moment you can't use your car anymore. **The bottom line is that our design ideas are broken. Our homes are unsuitable for where we are heading, and we don't have much time to fix it!**

But just pause for a moment, close your eyes, and envision this in your own community...

What if, with creative rezoning by jurisdictions, the empty Big Box store can become a Senior Community Center or Mature Market Apartments, and the asphalt jungle out front can be transformed into a walking park? This could become a "Naturally Occurring Retirement Community" (NORC) where, by definition, similarly aged people are attracted to and see the value of moving into a pocket neighborhood setting where they can be in a community of like-minded individuals. They see the chance to share a vision for living together and working as a team for the goal of increased longevity in their homes. Talk about a *win/win*! These commercial property locations are near health care, on the bus line, and have walking alternatives to restaurants and shopping too. This kind of experiment could kick-start the revitalization of the building industry in a down economy! It would require some proactive rezoning by jurisdictions across our country—jurisdictions that should be tired of the lack of tax revenue from empty buildings and failed businesses these last four or five years! I would think they should be interested in that, right?

Envision the vacant gas station as a Senior and Youth Center. Imagine the empty Kmart store renovated as a mixed-use building now, with a boutique retail multi-tenant storefront and independent living apartments above. This sounds a lot better than the sagging canopy and dirty concrete block building that's been vacant for the last four years, right? *Yes*, I agree.

I am aware that this would also require, as Louis Tenenbaum *would attest, the remainder of the "Full Systems Solution" approach. This is "big picture" planning that includes transit solutions, integration of health care to the home, food and meal solutions that work for the demographic, etc.* Louis Tenenbaum has been an aging in place leader and advocate for decades. He was instrumental in the authoring of literature by the MetLife Mature Market Institute titled "Aging In Place 2.0—Rethinking the Health Care Challenge."

If you are 40 or older, and especially if you are a true baby boomer, your actions as a consumer and the purchasing decisions you make *are driving the product development of the next 10 to 20 years.* So you are actively "casting votes" for the kind of world you want to live in, and you are leading the way for others.

I simply want to make a sincere and genuine *plea—a call to action.* Care enough about your future—and that of your loved ones—to imagine what it looks like in your own home and community, and to *plan for it*! We want clients, while they have the mental and physical faculties to do so, to be a part of their own solution. Unfortunate outcomes happen way too often, where someone has put off making these decisions, and then suddenly suffers an acute occurrence like a serious fall. Now one of their kids, from across the country, is making a choice for their parent's next living situation. "Oh, we don't have time to deal with it, but here's an assisted-living facility we found on the Internet within five miles of Mom's house." *Boom—that's your new home.* Regardless of a fall or illness, this outcome doesn't have to happen.

At some point in each of our lives, there *will be* a fork in the road, beyond which "planning ahead" is no longer possible. It's there, somewhere up ahead. I'd like to help you be on the fork that says "We planned ahead, this is perfect, and we've designed our 'forever home' to work for us for the rest of our lives."

Now, while you are capable of being in control of your decisions, do it! *Call* someone like ADM Architecture. *Do* an in-home assessment, even if you do the suggested alterations in phases. Change some door knobs to lever handles. Change some faucets to paddle operation versus twist and pull water supply handles. Add some task lighting. Remove some area rugs that are trip hazards. Pick up that "drop zone" you have on the stairs where you leave your books and clothes to go upstairs later. Do *something* to make your home work better. Start *somewhere*. Tackle the easy things first if you need to see results in little ways.

And start those valuable conversations with your loved ones. Begin addressing aging in place concerns. Contact some qualified professionals. And start to buy yourself and your loved ones some *real peace of mind about the future*. You will forever be glad that you did!

We all have to ENVISION. We have to THINK DIFFERENTLY. We have to SHARE our VISION with others, and do it with the PASSION that we can CHANGE THE WORLD. We have to start a REVOLUTION. Then, we can in fact do this... together. Accept responsibility for your life. Know that it is you who will get you where you want to go, no one else.
—Les Brown

If this book has been inspiring, interesting, and enlightening for you in some way, do us a favor: *Share it.* Send the information to a friend, family member, or loved one. We as a team can *magnify our voice.* We can educate the public, change the mentality, and inspire a paradigm shift that will benefit us all. Use your voice. Start the conversations we all need to be having with our own family and loved ones. Start the conversation with anyone and everyone who will listen! Your voice matters, so *please use it.*

Baby boomers have a huge voice as a demographic, and have the purchasing power as consumers to drive the demand that forces the supply to adjust accordingly. So make change happen by asking for it, demanding it, getting involved. Join civic groups and political movements. Write to your legislators: tell them this matters and that *you* matter. Tell them what *you* want and what you think is important. Tell them what you learned here in this book. Convey what we need to succeed in the decades ahead. State your desire to successfully age in place.

Let our builders and developers, our jurisdictions, and our elected officials know what we want for our lives, our homes, and our communities in the decades ahead. *Please don't wait*. The Silver Tsunami is here. It's crashing upon our shores. Get involved in planning your future, and the future of our great nation. Help design alterations to our existing housing stock, and help re-imagine the new homes for the future we are all facing. Voice your thoughts and opinions.

Share your hopes, fears, concerns, rights, needs, wishes, wants, and dreams. Every single proactive person helps to ***change the world.***

We can be reached in any of the following ways:

Empowering The Mature Mind

Website:

www.EmpoweringTheMatureMind.com

Email:

info@EmpoweringTheMatureMind.com

Facebook:

http://www.facebook.com/EmpoweringTheMatureMind

Twitter:

@AaronDMurphy

Radio Show "Encore Living" Website:

www.BlogTalkRadio.com/EncoreLiving

ADM Architecture

Website:

www.ADM-architecture.com

Email:

Aaron@ADM-architecture.com

Facebook:

http://www.facebook.com/ADMarchitecture

Acknowledgments:

THERE ARE SO MANY PEOPLE that have been instrumental in the vision, passion, focus, and confidence around the time and effort it took to tackle the authoring of my first book.

To my grandfather, Carl Murphy, thank you for being an idol for my entire life. As a product of the great depression, you were an amazing first boss on the Christmas tree farm, teaching me what a real work ethic looks like. And to see you happy and healthy, playing games with my own children at 93 years old in the fall of 2013, I continue to be inspired and blessed by you and your presence in all of our lives.

To my parents, Steve and Carol Murphy, I thank you for so many things. My thanks start with your conscious choice to save my life at birth, when in 1973 I was born at around 28-29 weeks and weighed under two pounds with a multitude of complications. You stood up for me then in the face of what appeared to be insurmountable adversity, and have stood behind me and beside me in support and encouragement ever since, in every single stage and challenge in my life. I can't thank you enough for your support in every single way, as words will never be enough. I can only try to live a life you'd be proud of, as a testament to your unparalleled support. I can't think of anyone I'd rather have that I can call than my folks. Thank you.

To my colleagues in architecture and the aging-in-place industry, thanks for your encouragement and cheerleading as I take on this personal journey of passion that is filled with free time in educating a nation on a topic I'm passionate about, while striving to make a living I can be proud of for my children and my family as an architect who can make lives better with the work I do. And also as an educator, a speaker, an author, a consultant, a mentor, and a business coach for others that want to succeed in this newly emerging industry space.

And a special thank you to my own mastermind group, where we meet each month to be accountable, transparent, emotional, and exposed about our strengths and our setbacks, all in the vein of intention for growth both personally and professionally. You are an amazing group of business owners, and I've learned so much about myself and my calling by spending regular time with you all.

And to one of those mastermind participants in particular, Mr. Samad Aidane, a gigantic thank you sir. You are the one who pulled me aside 3 years ago after seeing me speak to our Rotary club. You are the one who convinced me I had something special inside me. You are the one that told me in great detail why my message was so important to share, and that I was the right one to share that message with the world. You've been my biggest daily cheerleader, support network, and accountability partner for the last 3 years of this journey. You, my friend, are the spark of this passionate journey. You've fanned the fire as it sparked, and kept it going with me and for me through the entire process. I could never repay you for what you've done to get me where I am today, even if it was in great part behind the scenes and under the radar. Your own belief in me and this journey to sharing aging-in-place with the world has been a big part of the fuel for my fire, and I thank you from the bottom of my heart.

About the Author

AARON D. MURPHY is a businessman, an entrepreneur, and a philanthropist in his community. Aaron's career has been extensive and continuous in the fields of architecture and real estate for over 17 years. He has been a part of designing over one million square feet of commercial architecture projects during his career in the Seattle and western Washington, along with a multitude of residential projects. Aaron is a "Certified Aging-in-Place Specialist" (CAPS certification through NAHB) since 2009, and a licensed architect since 2003. He has been the owner of his own firm, ADM Architecture, since 2009.

Aaron has been public speaking on a regular basis for the last four years, with his most requested presentation being "The Aging In Place Phenomenon—How to Live Happily Ever After in Your Own Home". His presentations discuss the future of residential housing related to the bulging baby boomer population, and how we can live a longer, happier, and healthier life by staying in our own home as long as possible.

He has spoken to rooms of 250+ including mayors,

legislators, city council members, city and county planners, real estate developers, and real estate agents. He's also spoken to Rotary, Kiwanis, Lions, and similar clubs, as well as trade associations. Murphy has been interviewed for national publications and articles, as well as having been a regular contributing author to websites, blogs, magazines, and newspapers across the nation. He is a regular columnist in the publication "Encore Life Magazine" in the Seattle area (available online as well). He has also interviewed some of the nation's thought leaders in his industry, from Maryland to Texas to Portland, on the most timely, valid, and valuable topics related to the aging field and housing solutions. These interviews can be found as podcasts on the Empowering The Mature Mind website, along with their transcripts (upon request).

Based on his rising reputation as an expert in his field, Murphy was asked to bring his engaging presentation skills into co-hosting a live radio show called "Encore Living" in the Seattle, Washington, radio market, which launched in September 2012. The radio show started in the Seattle market on 1150am KKNW radio, and has recently changed to an internet format for a national platform and worldwide exposure. You can listen to the live show that he co-hosts every Tuesday morning at 9 a.m. Pacific Time, at BlogTalkRadio.com/EncoreLiving, along with his co-host and creator of the show, Mrs. Joyce Joneschiet, of Encore Living Interiors, a CAPS certified interior designer.

Who else is Aaron, when he's not at work?

"I love spending time with my beautiful kids, and getting outside with them (when our weather allows it) for some nature time and fresh air! Good parenting can be a full time job easily in its own right, and that keeps me pretty darn busy all by itself when I'm not at work.

Personal Mission Statement:

"With my strong desire for personal growth and knowledge, I strive to provide for myself and those around me an energetic and enjoyable environment for creating 'wealth' in all avenues of life. I act honestly and sincerely through a positive energy and strong worth ethic. I stay true to my beliefs and focus on the goals of fulfillment in the spiritual, physical, mental, emotional, and financial aspects of my own life and of the lives I come in contact with."

Statistics, Resources, and Credits:

AARP, "A State Survey of Livability Policies and Practices" by Nicholas Farber, Douglas Shinkle— National Conference of State Legislatures, Jana Lynott, Wendy Fox-Grage, Rodney Harrell, from: Public Policy Institute, December, 2011

http://www.aarp.org/home-garden/livable-communities/info-11-2011/Aging-In-Place.html

http://www.ncsl.org/documents/transportation/Aging-in-Place-2011.pdf

U.S. Census Data

http://www.census.gov/2010census/data/

http://www.census.gov/prod/cen2010/briefs/c2010br-03.pdf

U.S. Population Distribution by Age, 1950 through 2050

http://www.calculatedriskblog.com/2009/08/us-population-distribution-by-age-1950.html

Preparing for the Silver Tsunami

http://www.agingresearch.org/content/article/detail/826/

Falls Among Older Adults: An Overview

http://www.cdc.gov/homeandrecreationalsafety/falls/adultfalls.html

Centers for Disease Control and Prevention, National Center for Injury Prevention and Control.

Web–based Injury Statistics Query and Reporting System (WISQARS) [online]. Accessed November 30, 2010.

Americans Plan to Work Through Retirement

http://www.bankrate.com/finance/financial-literacy/americans-plan-to-work-through-retirement-1.aspx

Top 10 Trends in Senior Housing for 2012

http://seniorhousingnews.com/2012/01/09/top-10-trends-in-senior-housing-for-2012/

Home Modifications in the Elder Demographic

http://www.eldercare.gov/Eldercare.NET/Public/Resources/Factsheets/Home_Modifications.aspx

In Your Home ©Remodelors for Aging in Place, Facts & Statistics—According to research by the American Association of Retired Persons (AARP), www.aarp.org

http://www.iyhusa.com/AginginPlaceFacts-Data.htm

MetLife Mature Market Institute – Market Survey of Long-Term Care Costs

https://www.metlife.com/assets/cao/mmi/publications/studies/2011/mmi-market-survey-nursing-home-assisted-living-adult-day-services-costs.pdf

Aging in Place 2.0 MetLife Mature Market Institute: Rethinking Solutions to the Home Care Challenge

http://www.metlife.com/mmi/research/aging-in-place.html#insights

Exploring Senior Living Alternatives

http://www.purdue.edu/retirees/docs/SeniorLiving.pdf

Medical Bills Prompt More than 60 percent of U.S. Bankruptcies

http://articles.cnn.com/2009-06-05/health/bankruptcy.medical.bills_1_medical-bills-bankruptcies-health-insurance?_s=PM:HEALTH

Certified Aging-In-Place Specialist (CAPS)

http://www.nahb.org/page.aspx/category/sectionID=686

All About Aging Network

www.allaboutaging.org

National Aging In Place Council

www.naipc.org

Mature Market Institute

www.maturemarketinstitute.com

Alliance for Aging Research

www.agingresearch.org

National Alliance for Caregiving

www.caregiving.org